HAMLYN · COLOURFAX · SERIES

DINOSAUR & FOSSIL ACTIVITY BOOK

DOUGAL DIXON

CONTENTS

HAMLYN

THE KEY TO THE PAST

A fossil is any evidence, preserved in rock, of a plant or animal which was once alive. The creature may have lived many millions of years ago, and the fossil may be the remains of its shell (in the case of an animal such as a shellfish), its skeleton, or just the marks that showed where it once walked – a trail in solidified mud, frozen in time.

Dinosaurs were real, living animals that roamed the Earth between about 225 and 65 million years ago. Everything we know about dinosaurs has been learned from looking at fossils of one kind or another. Most fossils are the remains of animals which lived in water, especially the sea. Dinosaurs lived on land but, unfortunately, the dry conditions on land are not ideal for fossilization to occur. Therefore dinosaur fossils, such as a limb bone or a part of a skull, are very rare. You would be extremely lucky to find one. And, even if you do, you should take it to your local museum so that more can be learned about your find's origins. Indeed, if you want to see a dinosaur skeleton, the best place to go is to a natural history museum. Perhaps you could try to draw the skeleton, or imagine what the animal might have looked like when it was alive.

It has often been said that "the present is the key to the past". This means that, by looking at the way our natural world is today, we can learn more about the ways of the ancient world from the traces left behind in the rocks. And so it is with fossils. They can tell us what kinds of animals lived on Earth in the past, where they lived, how they lived and died, and so on. Even the rocks themselves can reveal a picture of what conditions were like all those millions of years ago. For example, a shale is a rock, made up of fine

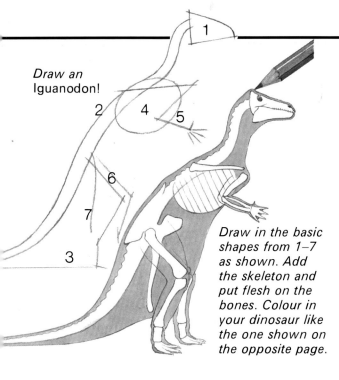

*Draw an
Iguanodon!*

*Draw in the basic
shapes from 1–7
as shown. Add
the skeleton and
put flesh on the
bones. Colour in
your dinosaur like
the one shown on
the opposite page.*

grains of mud which were deposited in
the sea. Many of the living things which
once inhabited our planet have died out,
but we know they existed because we can
find their fossilized remains.

The *Dinosaur and Fossil Activity Book*
has been specially written to help you
have fun finding out about dinosaurs and
other extinct animals. There are things to
make, projects to do and games to play.
The natural world, past and present, is a
very exciting place. You can never know
too much. To make the most of this book,
and to collect fossils, there are some items
of basic equipment which are useful to
have.

● For the book: *sand,
plaster of Paris powder,
plastic bottles, gravel,
some seashells, a cold-
casting resin hobby kit,
modelling clay and/or
plasticine, potatoes,
pencils, tracing paper,
some cardboard,
matchsticks, pipe-
cleaners, papier mâché,
small beads, pieces of
wire, some thread,
sketch pad, pencils,
coloured pencils,
crayons, or coloured
felt-tipped pens.*

Equipment you will need for the projects

Equipment you will need for fossil hunting

● For fossil hunting:
*strong boots or shoes,
outdoor clothing, a
sturdy bag for speci-
mens, notebook and
pencil, newspaper to
wrap your specimens, a
hand lens, a geological
hammer, a pair of
plastic goggles to
protect your eyes from
flying rock, chisels,
camera, geological map
and compass,
guidebook.*

WHAT IS A DINOSAUR?

The dinosaurs were a group of reptiles that lived for about 160 million years. They were very successful, and indeed, during their time on Earth they became the most powerful creatures alive. Dinosaurs were successful because there were many different kinds adapted to live in many different sorts of habitats and eat all kinds of food. Most other reptiles alive at the same time were unable to do this. Some dinosaurs were also very big and had horns or bony armour to protect themselves. Others were meat eaters.

The animals that we call dinosaurs were divided into two different groups. Scientists give these two groups special names – they call them the saurischians and the ornithischians. The names mean "the lizard-hipped animals" and the "bird-hipped animals". Some of the dinosaurs had hip bones like the hip bones of a lizard. The bones spread out in a star shape from the point where the leg was attached. The other group of dinosaurs had hip bones like the hip bones of a bird. The lower bones in this kind of hip were swept backwards. These descriptions do

The lizard-hipped Tyrannosaurus.

not mean lizard-hipped dinosaurs were the direct predecessors of lizards, however, nor that the bird-hipped dinosaurs were the direct predecessors of birds. In the pictures on this page the hip bones are shown coloured yellow, red, and blue.

Dinosaurs walked in a special way, quite unlike other reptiles, and the illustrations at the top of page 5 show you how and you can try and walk this way yourself. Lie down on your tummy on the floor. Now put your hands flat on the floor, wide apart, and stick out your elbows at the side. Push your body off the floor as if you are doing press-ups. Now try to walk like this. It is not easy, is it? This is how small reptiles, such as lizards, walk because their legs stick out at the sides.

Now move your hands right under your body and keep your arms straight. You will find this easier. This is the way that mammals walk. It is easier because your weight is being carried right down your arms, and your arms do not have to work

The bird-hipped Stegosaurus.

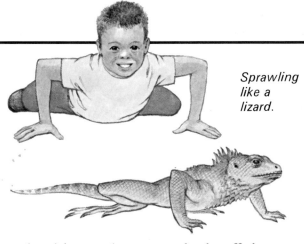

Sprawling like a lizard.

lived at the same time as the dinosaurs. There were crocodiles just like those of today. There were also pterosaurs – flying reptiles that had leathery wings. The crocodiles and the pterosaurs were close

so hard just to keep your body off the ground. Dinosaurs walked like this as well. They were very efficient animals for their time.

How do we know that dinosaurs walked like this? We can tell by the shape of the hips. An animal, such as a lizard, that has its legs sticking out at the sides, needs quite a firm joint where the leg is attached to the skeleton. The top of the leg bone is shaped like a ball, and it fits snugly into a rigid socket in the hips. This is a very strong arrangement. In a dinosaur's hip, there is no rigid socket between the hip bones and the leg, but there is a small shelf above it to stop the bone from jumping out.

OTHER REPTILES

There were other strange reptiles that

Now you are walking like a dinosaur.

relatives of the saurischians and ornithischians. All four groups developed earlier from the same group of small reptiles. There were also sea-living reptiles, such as the fish-shaped ichthyosaurs, the long-necked plesiosaurs, and the lizard-like mosasaurs. These were not related to the dinosaurs at all. They developed from totally different animals.

pterosaur

ichthyosaur

plesiosaur

mosasaur

Where did dinosaurs come from and what happened to them? Thousands of millions of years ago, the first kinds of animals appeared in the sea. With the passing of time, some of these animals altered, little by little, in shape, in habits, and in other ways to suit the changes that were taking place in their watery home. Those animals that did not change in ways which better suited their conditions, or those which changed in ways which made them less able to survive, slowly died out. In this way, animals – and plants – have been changing all the time and, of course, they are continuing to do so. We call this process evolution.

Many primitive sea animals resembled the kind of worm-shaped creature, with a mouth and eyes at one end, that you can roll out from modelling clay or plasticine. If you then flatten the tail end into a fin and pull fins out of the sides, you have a model which looks something like the first fishes. But fins are no use for walking on land. If you now make your fins into two pairs of legs and make the tail round again, you have the basic shape of a land animal such as an amphibian or reptile.

Dinosaurs developed from reptiles

Using modelling clay or plasticine, you can make a worm-like creature evolve into an amphibian.

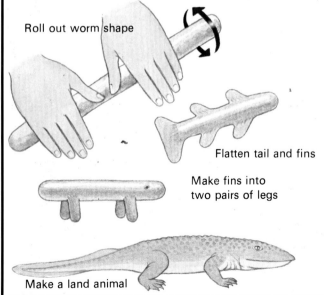

Roll out worm shape

Flatten tail and fins

Make fins into two pairs of legs

Make a land animal

called thecodonts (socket-toothed reptiles), which were sprawling crocodile-like animals that lived and hunted for food mainly in water. Gradually, over the aeons, they changed and many new kinds appeared so that, eventually, dinosaurs were the most successful animals on Earth. But, then, for reasons which are not fully understood, they died out quite suddenly.

GEOLOGICAL TIME SCALE

Scientists believe the Earth is about 4500 million years old, and they break down the history of the Earth into sections with different names. They call this the geological time scale. It shows the different periods of time, with their ages in millions of years.

You can make a mobile, using cut-out dinosaurs, to show when these animals lived in the geological time scale. Shown opposite are some dinosaurs. Trace them on to card and cut them out. Colour them the same colour as the periods on the time scale. For each animal shape cut a piece of thread 15 centimetres (6 inches) long and thread it through the hole in the shape. Now take all the shapes belonging to the Triassic period. (They should all be the same colour.) Attach the free ends of their threads to a piece of wire 30 centimetres (12 inches) long. Now do the same with all the Jurassic animals and all the Cretaceous animals.

Cut another thread about 40 centimetres (16 inches) long and attach it to the wire holding the Triassic animals so that the wire balances when you hold it by the thread. Attach a 30 centimetre (12 inch) thread to the Jurassic wire and allow this to balance, too. Finally, do the same with the Cretaceous wire using a 20 centimetre (8-inch) thread. If you attach the free ends of all these threads to another wire, you can then hang your mobile from the ceiling.

Cretaceous

Jurassic

Triassic

riceratops

Anatosaurus

Tyrannosaurus

finished mobile

Iguanodon

Stegosaurus

Diplodocus

Brachiosaurus

Plateosaurus

Lesothosaurus

Above: *The dinosaurs to use for your mobile*

7

THE BEAST-FOOTED DINOSAURS

The ancestors of the dinosaurs, the thecodonts, had long tails and long hind legs to help them to swim. When their descendants left the water to live on land, they found it easier to walk on their long hind legs, keeping their shorter front legs off the ground. The long tail was used as a "balancing pole". This is how the first, primitive dinosaurs walked.

You can make a model of a primitive dinosaur out of potatoes and pencils, like the one in the illustration. Take a medium-sized potato to use as a body. Stick a pair of pencils in one end to act as hind legs. Then stick potato halves on the ends of the pencils for feet. Cut a head out of cardboard and push it in at the shoulder region. The small front legs can be made from matchsticks. You will find that you will need a long pencil stuck in as a tail to balance all this. That is how all the meat-eating dinosaurs were built, too.

Scientists call the meat-eating dinosaurs theropods, meaning "beast footed". This is because the bones in the foot are arranged rather like those in a mammal's foot. They were one group of the lizard-hipped dinosaurs.

A potato and
pencils dinosaur

The skeleton shown here is of one of the biggest, Tyrannosaurus, which stood 6 metres (20 feet), showing how the body was designed. Next to it is a skeleton of one of the smaller dinosaurs, Coelophysis. It was only about 3 metres (10 feet) long, but it was built the same way. On the left are shown the bones in a dog's foot, for comparison.

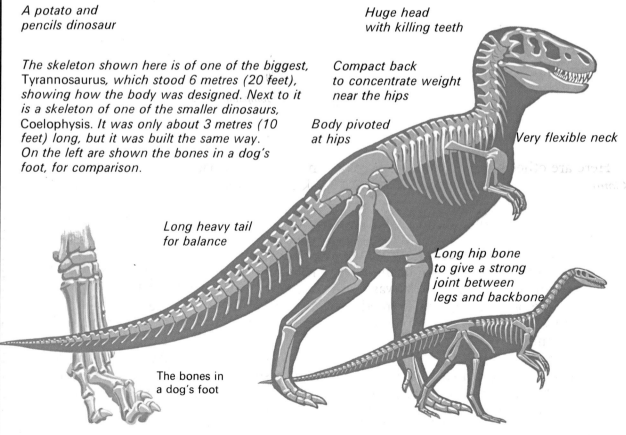

Huge head
with killing teeth

Compact back
to concentrate weight
near the hips

Body pivoted
at hips

Very flexible neck

Long heavy tail
for balance

Long hip bone
to give a strong
joint between
legs and backbone

The bones in
a dog's foot

Deinonychus hind foot

Baryonyx

Spinosaurus

Dilophosaurus

Compsognathus

Here are other beast-footed dinosaurs. *Compsognathus*. Late Jurassic, Germany. This was the smallest dinosaur known, about the size of a chicken. It chased and ate small lizards.

Deinonychus. Early Cretaceous, United States. *Deinonychus* must have been one of the fiercest of the meat eaters. It was about the size of a leopard and hunted the large plant-eating dinosaurs in packs, slashing them to death with the huge claw on the hind foot.

Dilophosaurus. Early Jurassic, United States. With a length of 6 metres (20 feet), this was a large but lightly built meat eater. It had a pair of crests on the skull that were probably used for signalling to mates or to enemies.

Spinosaurus. Late Cretaceous, North Africa. *Spinosaurus* was as big as *Tyrannosaurus*, but it had a huge sail or fin on its back. It probably used this sail to warm itself or to cool itself.

Baryonyx. Early Cretaceous, Britain. Unlike other beast-footed dinosaurs, this animal had strong forelimbs. It probably used the big claw on the hand to hook fish out of streams. It had a head like a crocodile, and many sharp teeth – ideal for eating fish.

THE LIZARD-FOOTED DINOSAURS

Some of the lizard-hipped dinosaurs became plant eaters. Plants are more difficult to digest than meat. Plant-eating animals need a much bigger gut or digestive system. Remake the model dinosaur

A potato and pencils dinosaur

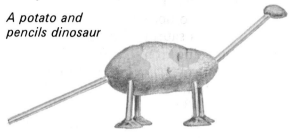

on page 8 but use a very long potato for the body. (The long body is needed to contain the long gut of a plant eater.) Make the front legs quite big, by using pencils.

You will find that no amount of weight on the tail will let this animal stand up on two legs. It would have to walk on all fours, even if it had a long tail. This four-legged animal would have been a much slower mover than a two-legged animal. Now give it a long neck so that it can reach around for its food without moving too far or too fast. This is how all the plant-eating, lizard-hipped dinosaurs were built.

Scientists call these big plant eaters sauropods, meaning "lizard footed", because the bones of the foot are arranged like those of a lizard.

Right: *Here is the skeleton of one of the longest,* Diplodocus, *to show how the bones were arranged*.

Long neck so that it can reach about for its food

Long body to hold the big digestive system

Deep hollows in the backbone, to keep the weight down

Four massive legs to support its weight

Long, thin tail to use as a whip against enemies

Right hind foot of *Diplodocus*

Right hind foot of *Anchisaurus*

Above: *This is the skeleton of* Anchisaurus – *a typical prosauropod.*

Long spines on the back and the base of the tail supported special back muscles. These enabled *Diplodocus* to rise on its hind legs to reach high into trees to find food, but for a short time only.

The lizard-footed dinosaurs evolved from the beast-footed dinosaurs. One group of dinosaurs – the prosauropods – show a half-way stage. They ate meat and plants, and could walk on two legs or four.

Here are some of the lizard-footed dinosaurs.

Brachiosaurus. Late Jurassic, North America and east Africa. *Brachiosaurus* was a very heavy and tall sauropod. Its front legs were longer than its hind legs, and it could stretch its neck upwards to a height of about 12 metres (40 feet). *Mamenchisaurus*. Late Jurassic, China. Half the 22-metre (72-feet) length of this animal was taken up by the neck. Otherwise, it was very similar to *Diplodocus*. *Opisthocoelicaudia*. Late Cretaceous, Mongolia. We do not know what the head and neck of this sauropod looked like – they were missing from the fossil. The whole animal would have been 12 metres (40 feet) long, and the tail was straight and held out stiffly behind. *Saltasaurus*. Late Cretaceous, Argentina. This was a rather unusual 12-metre-long (40-feet) sauropod in that its back was covered with armour.

Mamenchisaurus

Opisthocoelicaudia

Brachiosaurus

Saltasaurus

THE BIRD-FOOTED DINOSAURS

The bird-hipped dinosaurs were all plant eaters. The earliest of them could walk on their hind legs. Like all plant-eating animals, they needed a large gut. The different shape of hip bone meant that the gut could be held further back in the body than in the lizard-hipped dinosaurs.

Broad head with leaf-chewing teeth. The face had cheek pouches to help it to chew

Very flexible neck to reach food

Body balanced at the hips

Short, agile arms to help it to find food

Above: *The small, bird-hipped dinosaur shown here is* Hypsilophodon.

Lower back and tail stiffened to give rigid support at hips

Large gut suspended beneath the hips

Above: *Here is the skeleton of one of the biggest bird-hipped dinosaurs,* Edmontosaurus, *showing how it was arranged in real life*.

A potato and pencils dinosaur

You can make a potato model of a bird-hipped dinosaur, like you did with the lizard-hipped dinosaurs. Take a big potato for the body. Push the pencil legs into it about half way down. Now you can stick in the head, the front legs, and the tail. It will balance at the hips like the meat eaters. That is how some of the bird-hipped dinosaurs were built.

The smallest bird-hipped dinosaurs were so well balanced that they were fast runners. Scientists call these two-footed, bird-hipped dinosaurs ornithopods meaning "bird footed". That is because the bones of the foot were like those in the foot of a bird.

Here are some examples of bird-footed dinosaurs.

Scutellosaurus. Early Jurassic, south-west United States. This was a very small dinosaur, only about 1.2 metres (4 feet) long. It must have looked like a lizard and was covered with armour.

Ouranosaurus. Early Cretaceous, west Africa. This was about the size and shape of *Iguanodon* with a head like *Edmontosaurus*, but it had a tall ridge like a sail down its back. This may have been used to signal, or as a heat radiator.

Edmontosaurus belonged to a group called the duck-billed dinosaurs. Other duck-billed dinosaurs had crests on their heads.

Tsintaosaurus. Late Cretaceous, China. The crest of this duck-bill was like the horn of a unicorn, pointing upwards and forwards from between the eyes.

Pachycephalosaurus. Late Cretaceous, North America. This belonged to a group of dinosaurs called the "boneheads". There was a heavy mass of solid bone on the skull that may have been used as a battering ram. *Pachycephalosaurus* was the largest of them – about 5 metres (16½ feet) long.

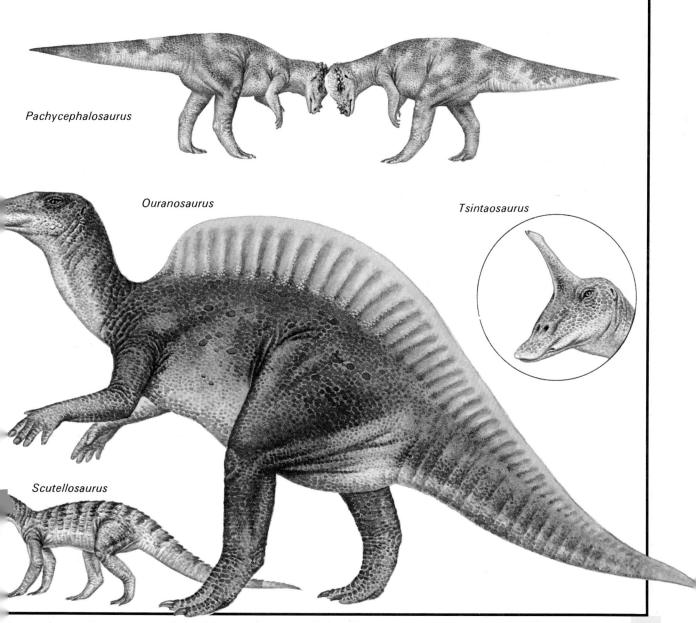

Pachycephalosaurus

Ouranosaurus

Tsintaosaurus

Scutellosaurus

THE ARMOURED DINOSAURS

Some of the later bird-hipped dinosaurs became armoured. Make some plates of armour from heavy cardboard and stick them on to your potato model of a basic bird-hipped dinosaur (see page 12). Soon you will have stuck so many pieces on that the model will fall over. That is why most of the armoured dinosaurs moved on four feet! Give your potato model four walking legs and try these sets of armour.

For the next design, stick armour plates along the back, pointing upwards. Stick some spikes on the tail as well to use as a weapon. Some dinosaurs had their back-bones protected like this.

Below: *This skeleton is of* Triceratops, *one of the biggest of the horned dinosaurs.*

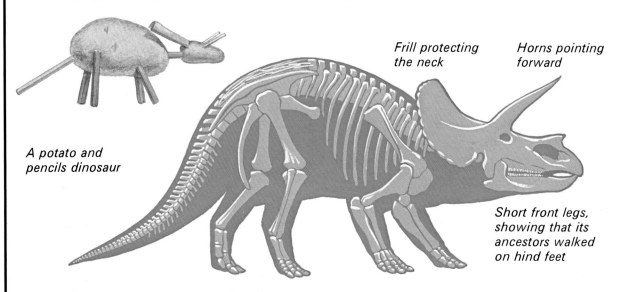

A potato and pencils dinosaur

Frill protecting the neck

Horns pointing forward

Short front legs, showing that its ancestors walked on hind feet

Stick a big armour plate on the head and put horns on it. You can do this with plasticine, modelling clay, or matchsticks. This kind of dinosaur could protect itself against enemies if it kept its head turned towards them. *Triceratops* was a horned dinosaur.

Below: *This* Stegosaurus *skeleton shows how the armour plates may have been arranged. This could not have been a very strong arrangement – the armour plates were not fixed to the skeleton.*

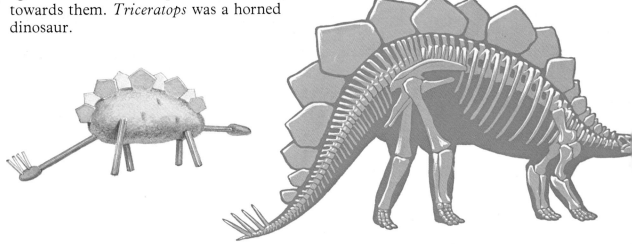

Psittacosaurus

Chasmosaurus

Scelidosaurus

Kentrosaurus

Here are some examples of armoured dinosaurs.

Psittacosaurus. Late Cretaceous, China. This 1-metre-long (4-foot) dinosaur was really the ancestor of the horned dinosaurs, although it had no horns. The ridges at the back of the head supported the jaw muscles and these later became the neck frill.

Chasmosaurus. Late Cretaceous, North America. This had an enormous neck shield that was probably used for signalling, as well as for defence.

Kentrosaurus. Late Jurassic, east Africa. This was closely related to *Stegosaurus* but, instead of plates, it had spikes all down its back. It was about 5 metres (16½ feet) long.

Scelidosaurus. Early Jurassic, Britain. This 3.5-metre-long (11½-foot) dinosaur was one of the first of the armoured types. It was probably the ancestor of the heavy animals like *Euoplocephalus*.

For the last design, arrange the armour plates so that they are lying flat against the back. Stick them on to the potato with sticky tape. Put a small potato on the end of the tail to act as a club. *Euoplocephalus*, one of the last of the armoured dinosaurs (shown below) was protected like this.

Euoplocephalus

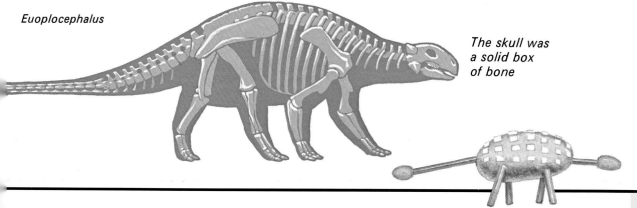

The skull was a solid box of bone

WHERE DO YOU FIND FOSSILS?

Fossils are found in sedimentary rocks. These are rocks which are made from the kinds of sediments, such as sand and mud, that once built up in layers on the bottom of a lake or the sea. As more and more layers built up, the weight of the sediments on top squeezed out the water from those below. Finally, the individual grains were cemented together by natural chemicals called minerals, and a sedimentary rock was formed. After the rocks have formed, and as the Earth's land masses drift and slowly grind together, the rocks can be pushed up as mountains. This is called mountain building and is the reason why rocks that were formed in the sea are now found on dry land.

When an animal dies, its remains, that is, its flesh and any hard parts, such as a skeleton or a shell, usually rot or are broken up. Sometimes, though, part of the animal may be preserved as a fossil. Sea creatures, such as cockles which have hard shells, eventually die. The flesh rots but the shell might be buried in the sediment at the bottom of the sea before it is broken up. Then it can be preserved as a fossil in rock. Or an insect might get trapped in the sticky resin that oozes from certain kinds of trees. If this resin is preserved, the insect is preserved in amber. Sometimes, it is just the outlines of leaves, or the tracks of an animal walking across soft mud, that are preserved as fossils.

Because most sedimentary rocks form at the bottom of the sea, most fossils are sea creatures. Dinosaurs lived on land, of course, so their fossils are rare. Their remains might have been fossilized if they fell into a river and drowned so that they were then washed into the sea, or if a river flooded and spread sediments over the land. Different kinds of rocks can also tell you quite a lot about the conditions which existed at the time when the rock was formed. For example, even the shapes

The base of a cliff at the seaside may be a good place to look for fossils.

of sand dunes can be preserved in sedimentary rocks called sandstones to show that desert dunes were once being slowly blown across the landscape.

You can find fossils for yourself, especially fossils of sea creatures such as ammonites or cockle-like animals. You might even find the teeth of extinct sharks. Old road and railway cuttings, river beds, sea cliffs, quarries, on shingle beaches, even freshly ploughed fields, can all hold fossils.

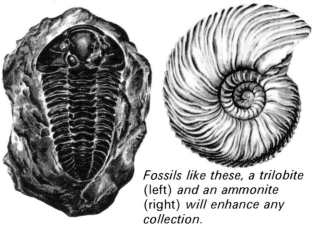

Fossils like these, a trilobite (left) *and an ammonite* (right) *will enhance any collection.*

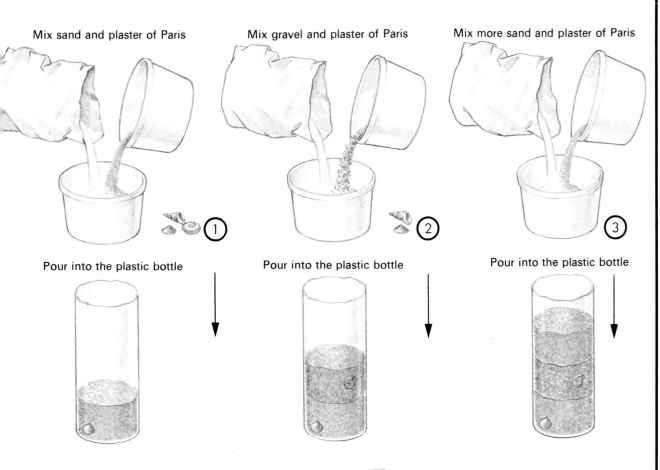

Mix sand and plaster of Paris

Mix gravel and plaster of Paris

Mix more sand and plaster of Paris

① ② ③

Pour into the plastic bottle

Pour into the plastic bottle

Pour into the plastic bottle

Try making your own fossil-rich sedimentary rock. Mix about a cupful of sand with the same amount of plaster of Paris powder. Pour it into a plastic bottle. Do the same with some gravel. Then again with more sand so that you have different layers in your bottle like layers of sediment. As you pour in the layers, put in some seashells. Pour in some water and leave it to stand overnight. Next day, you will find that all the sand and gravel has cemented together just like a sedimentary rock. Split open the bottle and break your rock with a geological hammer. You should find your seashells embedded in the rock like fossils.

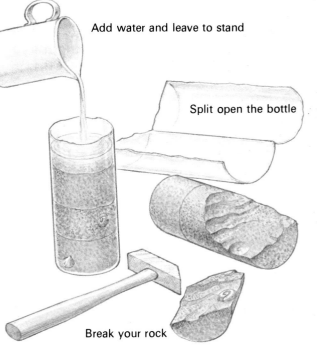

Add water and leave to stand

Split open the bottle

Break your rock

Fossil hunting

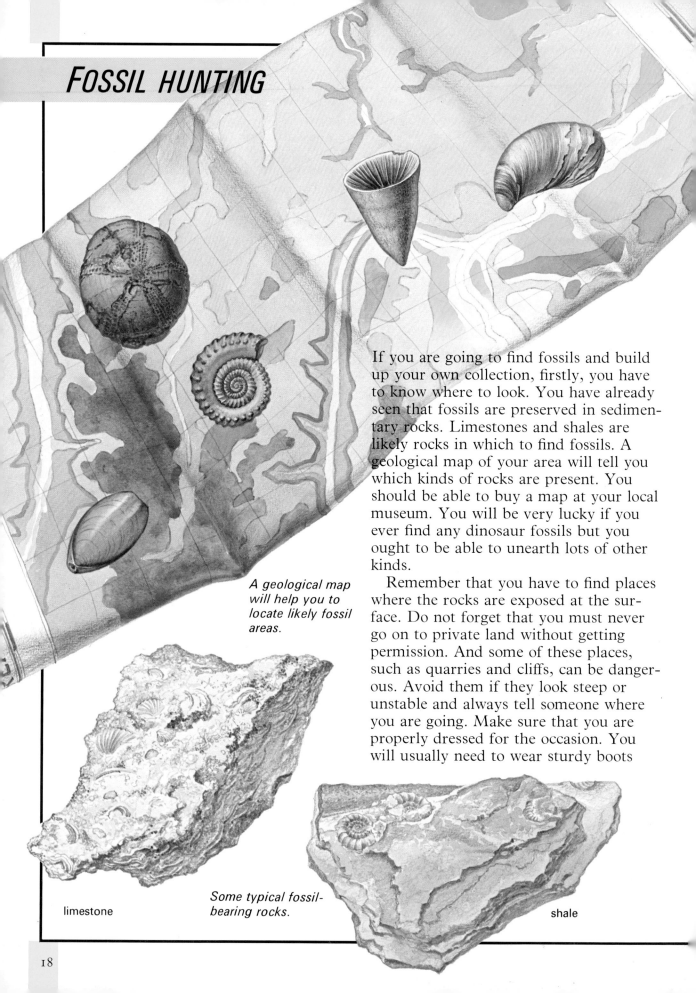

A geological map will help you to locate likely fossil areas.

Some typical fossil-bearing rocks.

limestone

shale

If you are going to find fossils and build up your own collection, firstly, you have to know where to look. You have already seen that fossils are preserved in sedimentary rocks. Limestones and shales are likely rocks in which to find fossils. A geological map of your area will tell you which kinds of rocks are present. You should be able to buy a map at your local museum. You will be very lucky if you ever find any dinosaur fossils but you ought to be able to unearth lots of other kinds.

Remember that you have to find places where the rocks are exposed at the surface. Do not forget that you must never go on to private land without getting permission. And some of these places, such as quarries and cliffs, can be dangerous. Avoid them if they look steep or unstable and always tell someone where you are going. Make sure that you are properly dressed for the occasion. You will usually need to wear sturdy boots

because you will often have to tramp

because you will often have to tramp across rough country. In areas where it is likely to be wet or cold, you should always have plenty of warm, waterproof clothing. But, in other places, where it might be hot and dry, you should try to keep cool and shaded from the sun. And you should always have plenty of water to drink.

You already know what kind of equipment you will need for a fossil-hunting expedition but how do you go about finding your first fossil? Suppose you are on a beach and you have found a likely-looking boulder of limestone. It will probably be weathered and dirty on the surface. This is where your geological hammer is needed to break open the rock and reveal the fresh rock and fossils inside. But take care when you break rocks. Always wear a pair of goggles to protect your eyes from flying splinters of rock. Chisels can also help to extract fossils. Or in soft, muddy rocks, you will find a simple trowel helpful. And don't just go around smashing every rock you see or digging out huge holes in soft cliffs. If you do, you can cause a lot of damage, and valuable fossils might be destroyed. It might be better to photograph your site. Always take a note of where you find things. Wrap up your specimens in newspaper to carry them home.

MAKING A COLLECTION

When you get home, you should label every fossil you have found, and also make a catalogue of your collection. Your catalogue could be in a notebook, but a simple card index might be better. It should tell you where you found the fossil, when, and in what kind of rock it was preserved. If you cannot identify it (and there are many books to help you), take it to your local museum. Someone should be able to help. Write the name of the fossil on its label and in your catalogue.

You can keep your collection in special storage cabinets which you can buy or which you can make for yourself. Look at the ones in the museum as a guide, or get someone to help you. In time, you may be able to build up a valuable collection. Remember, too, that amateur fossil hunters sometimes make important discoveries.

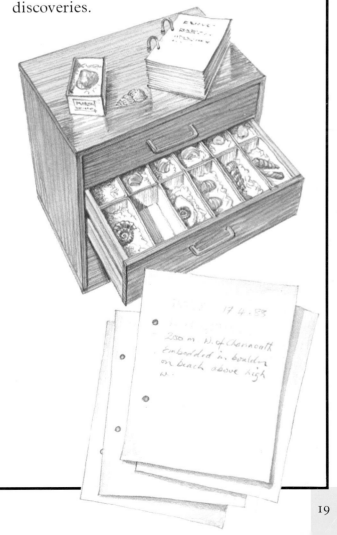

MODEL DINOSAURS

How do we know what dinosaurs looked like? We only have their skeletons originally in the form of fossilized bones to help us.

If the complete skeleton is preserved, then it is easy to build it up as it was in real life. Scientists sometimes mount them in museums in life-like poses. A display like this is called a **reconstruction**. More often, the bones are taken to the museum in the slab of rock as they are found and put on display just like that.

Trace round the bones that are scattered on this page. You will need to draw some of the bones more than once, so copy them by the number of times indicated. Make holes in the bones where shown. Now you can fix the bones together to make the complete skeleton shown at the bottom of the page. Join the bones with thread. If you wish, you can glue the completed skeleton on to card in a lifelike pose. Then transfer the shapes to stiff card and cut them out.

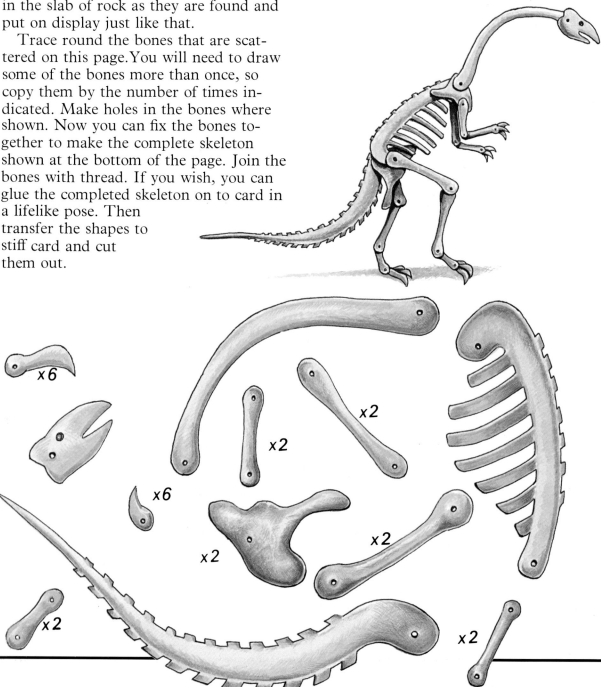

x6

x2

x2

x6

x2

x2

x2

x2

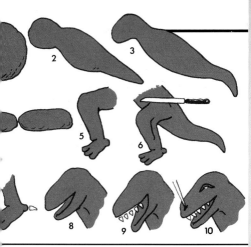

The finished model looks like this – of course you can vary the colours!

MAKING A FRAME DINOSAUR

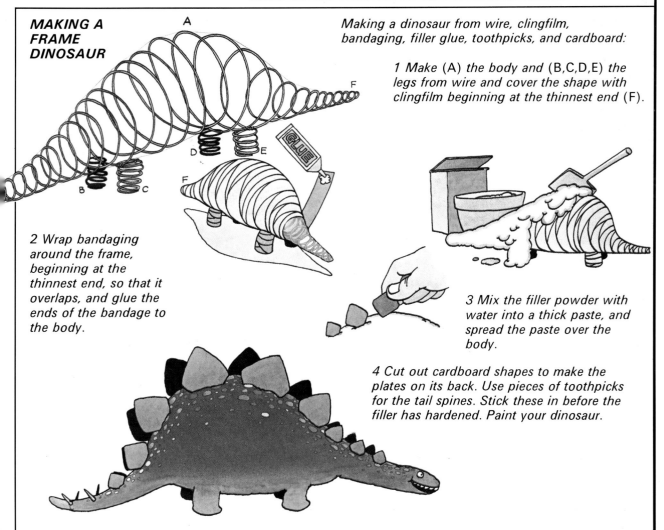

Making a dinosaur from wire, clingfilm, bandaging, filler glue, toothpicks, and cardboard:

1 Make (A) the body and (B,C,D,E) the legs from wire and cover the shape with clingfilm beginning at the thinnest end (F).

2 Wrap bandaging around the frame, beginning at the thinnest end, so that it overlaps, and glue the ends of the bandage to the body.

3 Mix the filler powder with water into a thick paste, and spread the paste over the body.

4 Cut out cardboard shapes to make the plates on its back. Use pieces of toothpicks for the tail spines. Stick these in before the filler has hardened. Paint your dinosaur.

RESTORING A DINOSAUR

Sometimes it is possible to find complete skeletons of dinosaurs which, even though the bones have become separated, can be

Try restoring any kind of dinosaur following the method shown here.

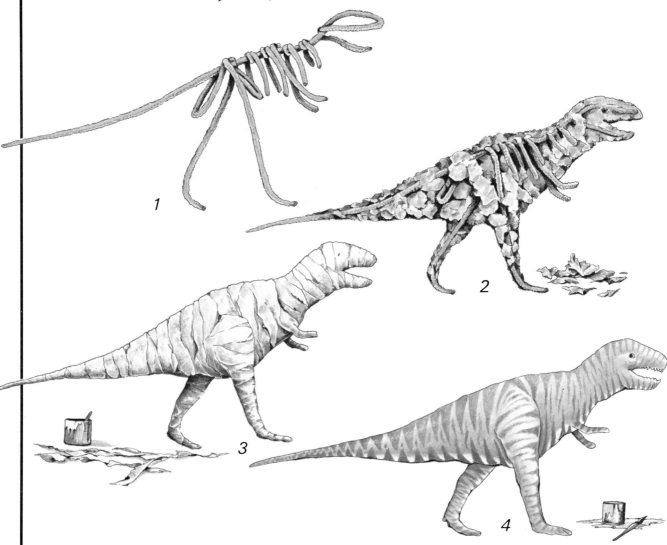

1

2

3

4

pieced together into a reconstruction. Even if not all the bones are preserved, scientists can make use of the ones they have and then produce a drawing of the whole skeleton.

If you have read other books on dinosaurs, you may have wondered how we are able to suggest what the whole animal looked like. In other words, how do scientists put flesh on the bones to make what is known as a **restoration**? By looking at marks on individual dinosaur bones, a

scientist can decide where the animal's muscles were attached. From this, he or she can build up a picture of the flesh of the animal. Of course, knowing about the anatomy of modern animals helps in this. Then the scientist can guess at what the skin was like and even what colour the animal might have been. Often the scientist then asks a skilled artist to draw an impression of the dinosaur. Sometimes, artists make models of the animals instead. You can do this yourself (*see* above).

Take some pipe cleaners (1) and build a model of one of the dinosaur skeletons on pages 8–15. Twist several pipe cleaners together to make the backbone strong. Now cover it with muscles made from papier mâché (2). Mix some cold-water wallpaper paste and tear some newspaper into strips. Coat the paper strips with paste and wind them around the bones (3) until you build up a good thickness, especially around the legs, neck, and tail. You do not need to fill the space between the ribs with papier mâché. There would be no flesh here, but you can imagine that this is where the lungs, the heart, the intestines, and all the other organs would be. You could make the insides out of coloured modelling clay but, of course, you will not see them when your model is finished.

Wait for your first layer of papier

mâché – the flesh layer – to dry. Then tear some small pieces of newspaper, paste them, and cover the whole model to produce a smooth layer of "skin". Make eyes from small beads and, if your animal is a meat eater, make teeth from stiff paper or matchsticks. If it is armoured, cut the armour pieces from stiff card.

When it is dry, paint your animal (4) with poster paints. Try to imagine the colour it would have been. For example, a very big animal could have drab colours. A small animal might be quite bright. Compare a little lizard with a crocodile. Fierce, hunting animals might have been striped or spotted like tigers or leopards. Plant-eating animals might have been camouflaged like modern deer. Any big frills or crests might be brightly coloured so that they can be used as signals, like the bright colours of a modern peacock.

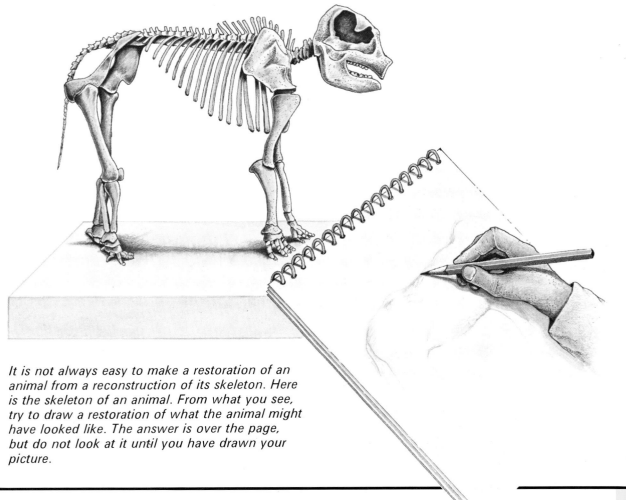

It is not always easy to make a restoration of an animal from a reconstruction of its skeleton. Here is the skeleton of an animal. From what you see, try to draw a restoration of what the animal might have looked like. The answer is over the page, but do not look at it until you have drawn your picture.

HEADS AND BODIES

Why is there an elephant on this page? It is the answer to the puzzle at the end of page 23. Did you manage to restore it?

The trunk is made of muscle, with no bones in it, and so there is no sign of a trunk on the skeleton. We took the tusks off, because, being teeth, they would probably have fallen out before the skeleton fossilized. These are the kind of things that would have been difficult to tell from the fossilized skeleton.

1 Look at the fierce teeth in this head. They must have been used for tearing into flesh.

We have seen that most dinosaur skeletons are found incomplete. Usually they are missing the skull. Here is a picture of a dinosaur skull. It belonged to a meat-eating dinosaur called *Allosaurus*. You can see how it is made up of thin strips of bone. Skulls like this usually fall to pieces before they are fossilized.

Here are some dinosaurs heads and bodies for you to match up. Note that they are not all to the same scale. (The answers are given on page 32.)

A

This animal was a big plant eater. It had a very long neck. It must have had a very small head or the neck would never have bee able to support it.

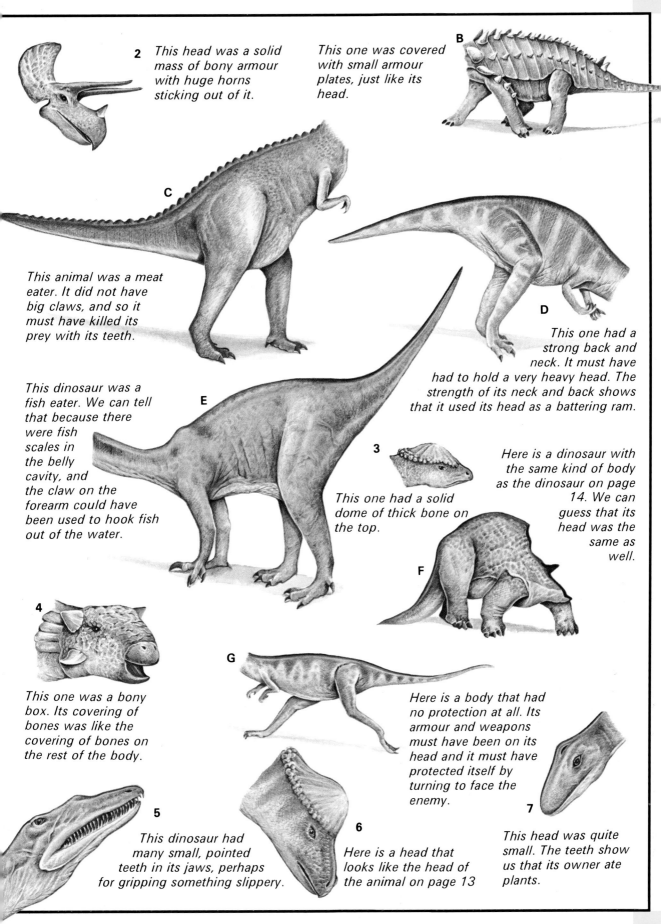

2 This head was a solid mass of bony armour with huge horns sticking out of it.

This one was covered with small armour plates, just like its head.

B

C

This animal was a meat eater. It did not have big claws, and so it must have killed its prey with its teeth.

D

This one had a strong back and neck. It must have had to hold a very heavy head. The strength of its neck and back shows that it used its head as a battering ram.

This dinosaur was a fish eater. We can tell that because there were fish scales in the belly cavity, and the claw on the forearm could have been used to hook fish out of the water.

E

3

This one had a solid dome of thick bone on the top.

Here is a dinosaur with the same kind of body as the dinosaur on page 14. We can guess that its head was the same as well.

F

4

This one was a bony box. Its covering of bones was like the covering of bones on the rest of the body.

G

Here is a body that had no protection at all. Its armour and weapons must have been on its head and it must have protected itself by turning to face the enemy.

7

5

This dinosaur had many small, pointed teeth in its jaws, perhaps for gripping something slippery.

6

Here is a head that looks like the head of the animal on page 13

This head was quite small. The teeth show us that its owner ate plants.

There is a certain kind of fossil called a **trace fossil**. This represents a trace of where an animal has been. Worm burrows and centipede tracks can be trace fossils. Dinosaurs leave trace fossils as well, in the form of footprints. Dinosaur footprints are usually more common than dinosaur bones. You can easily see why. One dinosaur will leave millions of footprints behind it throughout its life, but only one skeleton.

Meat-eating theropod dinosaurs walked on two legs. We have known that for a long time. Above are some trackways made by meat-eating dinosaurs. You can make your own dinosaur footprints.

On these pages is the shape of a meat-eating dinosaur's footprint. It has three toes and long claws. Scale up this shape and transfer it on to plywood or chipboard. Cut it out, or get someone to do it for you. Do this twice so that you have a pair of dinosaur feet. Drill holes in them and tie them to your own feet with string.

Now walk along a sandy beach and see what kind of track you can make. To get the kind of track scientists have found, you will have to walk with bandy legs.

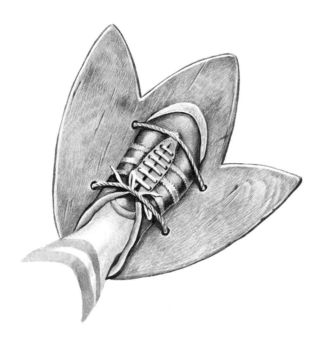

feet in as they went.

The footprint shapes below are the shapes of the feet of sauropod dinosaurs – the big plant eaters with the long necks. The big one is the hind foot. The small one is the front foot. You can make sauropod footprints the same way as you made the theropod prints. Fix the big ones to your own feet. Fix the small ones to sticks and hold these in your hands. Now walk along the sandy beach supporting your forequarters on the sticks. See how the hind feet tend to walk all over the prints of the front feet. We see this in fossil footprints as well.

Does this mean that the meat-eating dinosaurs walked with bandy legs? The scientists who studied those tracks then found that eventually they were really two sets of tracks! If you and a friend walked side by side you would make the same tracks. The dinosaurs that made these tracks must have been walking side by side. What is more, they must have been taking very small steps, and turning their

Just look at the size of the man compared with this sauropod. You can see why you need to scale up the size of the footprints!

DINOSAUR NESTS

In 1922 an American expedition went into the depths of the Gobi desert in Asia. It was called the Central Asiatic Expedition and was led by the scientist, Roy Chapman Andrews. They were actually looking for fossil humans. They found fossil dinosaurs instead.

They also found dinosaur nests – the first known to science. Each nest had about thirty eggs. Each egg was about 20 centimetres (8 inches) long and 7 centimetres (2¾ inches) in diameter. They were laid in a spiral pattern. The nests were made by a 2-metre-long (6½-foot) dinosaur called *Protoceratops*.

You can make your own *Protoceratops* nest. Take a number of standard-sized plastic lemonade bottles – the ones with the cup on the bottom to make them stand up. You do not need thirty but get as many as you can. Take the cups off. The bottles are now about the same size and shape as *Protoceratops* eggs. Paint them white.

Now arrange them in a sandpit or a hole in the beach. Put them in a circle, with the cap end pointing inwards and downwards so that we won't see it. Then put another ring of "eggs" on top of them, and so on until they are all used. Scatter sand over them so that they are partly covered. That is what a *Protoceratops* nest would have looked like.

Now make a model of a *Protoceratops* baby inside the egg. The picture shows what a baby *Protoceratops* looked like. Take 1.5 kilograms (just over 3 pounds) of plasticine or modelling clay and make a baby *Protoceratops*. Use marbles for the eyes – they would be about the right size. Cut the top off an unpainted lemonade bottle. Now push your baby *Protoceratops* in so that it fills it. Do not worry if it bends and distorts – a baby animal in the egg is often very cramped up anyway. From a baby the size of this grew an adult *Protoceratops* 2 metres (6½ feet) long.

Roy Chapman Andrews and some colleagues examining a Protoceratops *nest in the Gobi Desert.*

The female Protoceratops *laid her eggs in a shallow pit in the sand. She probably then covered the eggs with sand. Notice the small dinosaur in the distance. This dinosaur was called*

Oviraptor. *Its skeleton was found in a* Protoceratops *nest. It was probably trying to steal the eggs.*

How to make your own dinosaur eggs using plastic lemonade bottles.

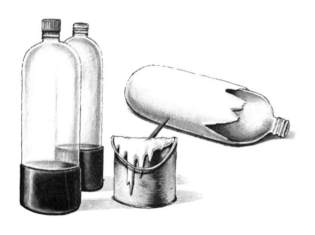

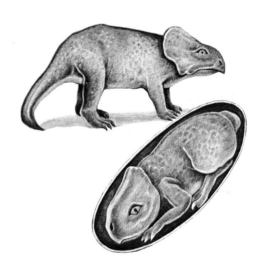

OTHER NESTS

Since then many other dinosaur nests have been found. In Montana, USA, and Alberta, Canada, there have been found fossil nests of duck-billed dinosaurs such as the species called *Maiasaura*. They were originally heaps of mud 3 metres (10 feet) in diameter, and 1.5 metres (5 feet) high. The eggs were laid in a depression at the top of this in a hollow 2 metres ($6\frac{1}{2}$ feet) wide and 0.75 metres ($2\frac{1}{2}$ feet) deep.

Make a model Protoceratops *out of plasticine or modelling clay. Push it into the plastic bottle. This is how the baby dinosaur would have looked in real life.*

Many duck-bills nested at the same site, and came back year after year to the same place. Young duck-bills were found in the nests as well, showing that the parents must have looked after them for some time after they had hatched – just like parent birds.

A DINOSAUR LANDSCAPE

Fill a shallow wooden tray (about the size of a tea tray) with sand to resemble a desert. You can make a ''waterhole'' by cutting out from aluminium foil a roughly circular shape. Some small pebbles and bits of grass could make rocks and shrubs around the pond.

Now you need to give your scene a backdrop. Cut out a rectangle of card to fit the back of your tray as shown in the diagram on the right. Fold it in two places so that it can be shaped around the sides of the tray, too. Paint the card with the scene shown here but without the dinosaurs. Fold the backdrop around the tray. You now have your dinosaur landscape and you just need some dinosaurs.

Simply, draw a graph of evenly sized squares (of the right proportion to fit your scene) and copy the dinosaurs square by square. Cut them out leaving tabs at the bottom to push into the sand, and paint them to make them look realistic. Instead, you can just trace out the dinosaurs in the top picture.

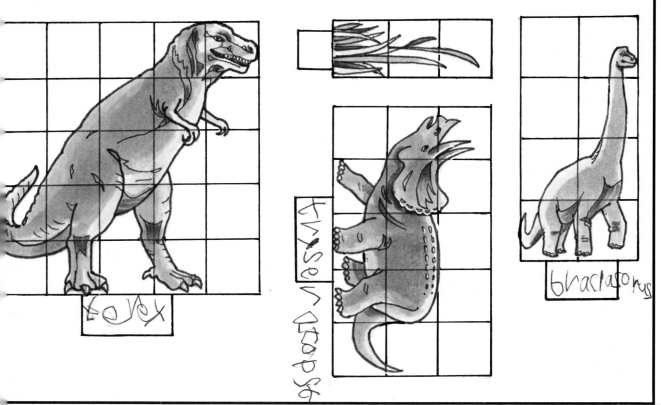

t-rex

triceratops

brachiasorus

Index

Answer to puzzle p.25:

Matching the dinosaur heads and bodies.

1C *Tyrannosaurus*
2F *Triceratops*
3G *Stegoceras*
4B *Euplocephalus*
5E *Baryonyx*
6D *Pachycephalosaurus*
7A *Diplodocus*

Published in 1988 by
The Hamlyn Publishing Group Limited
a division of Paul Hamlyn Publishing
Michelin House, 81 Fulham Road, London SW3 6RB

Copyright © The Hamlyn Publishing Group Limited 1988

ISBN 0 600 55534 8

Printed and bound in Italy
Front jacket illustration: Anthony Morris, Anwar Islam, National Trust
Photographic Library
Illustrations: Denys Ovenden, Eric Robson, Simon Burr, Victor Ambrus
Editorial and design: Curtis Garratt Limited
General editor: Derek Hall
Dinosaur model: Derek Hall